CASTLES

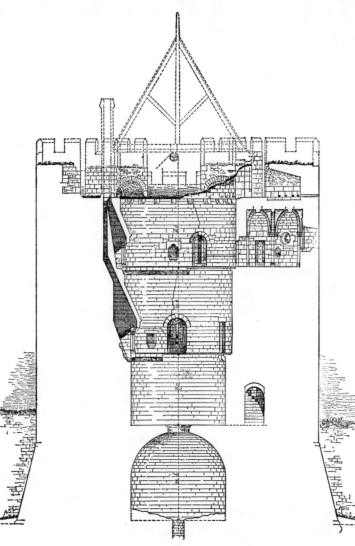

Inside a keep or donjon (Conisborough)

Text by J. K. Anderson

Models by Nick Taylor

The White Tower

William the Conqueror held England in a network of castles, some belonging to the Crown and commanded by the King's own officers, some to the great lords who held land directly from the King, some to the lesser barons. Forty-nine castles are actually named in Domesday Book, the great survey of the kingdom that was made near the end of the Conqueror's reign, and most of these had been built since the Conquest. But there were many others which were not mentioned, including the greatest of them all, the Tower of London.

When London submitted to the Normans in 1066, shortly after the Battle of Hastings, the City was still defended by "London Wall," the line of Roman fortifications running in a rough semicircle from Blackfriars to Billingsgate, with its ends resting upon the River Thames. Westminster, with its great church and palace, higher up the Thames and on the same bank as the city, had already been established by Edward the Confessor (who died there), but William determined to secure the City itself by a fortress which should command the approach up-river and the Pool of London, the greatest seaport in the Kingdom, where shipping lay at anchor below London Bridge.

This first castle seems to have been formed of earthworks and palisades enclosing the south-east corner of the Roman fortifications. In other places, notably at Pevensey and Porchester, the Normans built castles within the walls of Roman fortresses, which are standing to this day. At London the Roman fortifications have been demolished, but they were remembered, and poets claimed that the Tower had been built by Julius Caesar himself —

> By Julius Caesar thy tower founded of old
> May be the mount of Mars majesticall,
> Whose artillerie with tongue may not be told.
> London, thou art the flower of cities all.

Or, less appreciatively,

> Ye Towers of Julius, London's lasting shame,
> With many a foul and midnight fed.

But in actual fact the oldest part of the Tower, and the one that gives its name to the whole, is the great Norman donjon, the White Tower, so called because during the Middle Ages it was regularly whitewashed, as can be seen from a famous picture showing Charles Duke of Orleans, held captive in the Tower for many years after the Battle of Agincourt in 1415.

The White Tower was probably begun in about 1077, under the direction of Gundulf of Bec, a Norman priest who became Bishop of Rochester and a famous builder. William Rufus, the Conqueror's son, who ruled from 1087 to 1100, pushed the work on, and seems also to have built a palace and a high wall surrounding the whole. The great fortress, "built with mortar tempered with the blood of beasts," was hated by freedom-loving Londoners, especially as they were heavily taxed to pay for it. So when Rufus was murdered one of the first acts of his brother, Henry I, was to imprison Ralph Flambard, the man responsible for the building and the taxes. But Flambard was given a handsome allowance to buy food and drink. One of the barrels of wine that was brought in to him had a long rope coiled inside it. First he made his guards drunk with the wine, then he climbed down the rope and escaped to the riverside, where a ship was waiting to take him to Normandy. (Afterwards the King forgave him and he came back to his Bishopric of Durham and became a great castle-builder in the North of England.)

Ralph Flambard was the first state prisoner in the Tower, and the first to escape from it. Not all were as fortunate. In 1244 the Welsh Prince Gruffydd tried to let himself down from the roof of the White Tower by a rope made of knotted bedclothes, which broke just after he had started. He fell ninety feet, and "his head and neck were crushed between his shoulders."

The White Tower is not quite square in plan, and measures on the outside 107 feet, north and south, by 118 east and west. The walls are between twelve and fifteen feet thick, and strengthened on the outside by flat buttresses. At the north-east corner is a rounded turret, with a spiral staircase inside it, and at the south-east the wall curves outward in a bow, to make room for the rounded apse of the little Chapel of Saint John, in the third storey. There are more spiral staircases in the thickness of the wall in the other two corners, and at all four corners turrets rise above the line of

The White Tower

2. Fold Wall as shown; cement to Top Wall by first cementing ends, then center each raised part over a flap & cement

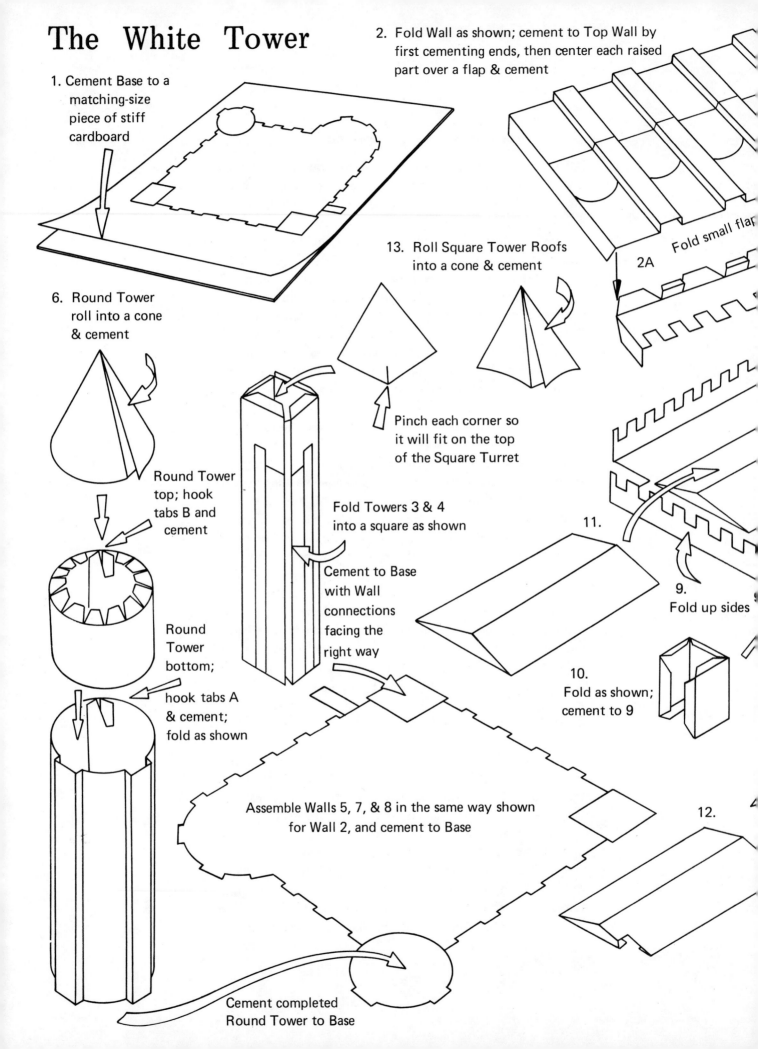

1. Cement Base to a matching-size piece of stiff cardboard

Fold small flap

2A

13. Roll Square Tower Roofs into a cone & cement

6. Round Tower roll into a cone & cement

Pinch each corner so it will fit on the top of the Square Turret

Round Tower top; hook tabs B and cement

Fold Towers 3 & 4 into a square as shown

Cement to Base with Wall connections facing the right way

11.

9.
Fold up sides

Round Tower bottom;

hook tabs A & cement; fold as shown

10.
Fold as shown; cement to 9

Assemble Walls 5, 7, & 8 in the same way shown for Wall 2, and cement to Base

12.

Cement completed Round Tower to Base

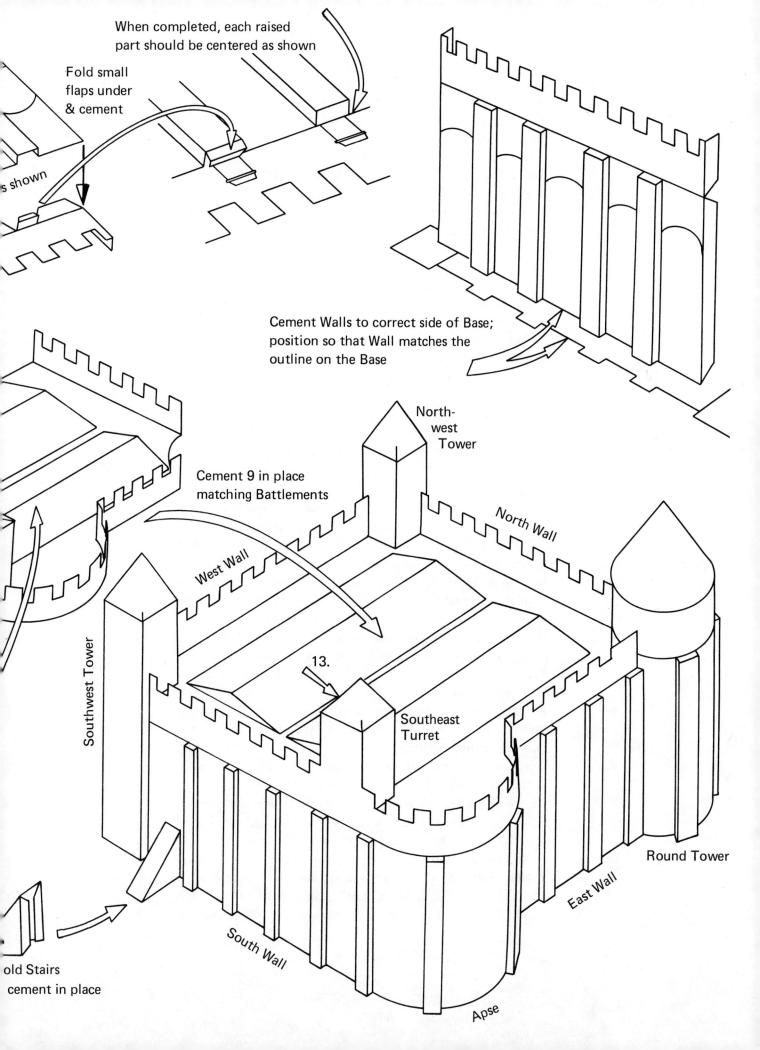

When completed, each raised part should be centered as shown

Fold small flaps under & cement

s shown

Cement Walls to correct side of Base; position so that Wall matches the outline on the Base

Cement 9 in place matching Battlements

North-west Tower

North Wall

West Wall

13.

Southwest Tower

Southeast Turret

Round Tower

East Wall

South Wall

Apse

old Stairs cement in place

the battlements. In Charles II's time the north-east turret was for a time fitted out as an observatory for Flamsteed, the famous Astronomer Royal. The Prime Meridian, from which the degrees of longitude all round the earth are calculated, would have passed through the White Tower, if the smoke from the "sea-coal" shipped from Newcastle and the "London particular" fogs had not made it desirable to move the observatory to Greenwich.

The inside of the Tower was planned in four storeys. Probably the original entrance was one floor up, on the south, and the basement could only be reached from above. It was divided into three large rooms—store-rooms, and in the south-east corner a dark prison known as "Little Ease."

The other storeys were arranged in the same way—cut in half by a thick wall running from north to south, with the western half left as a single large chamber, and the eastern half divided into two unequal parts by a cross-wall. There were fireplaces on the second and third floors, which must have been used for living accommodation, and the cold, inconvenient, dark, gloomy rooms were probably subdivided with wooden partitions, in spite of the risk of fire. But the "Council Chamber," which occupies the western half of the top floor, and the "Banqueting Chamber," the north-eastern room of the third storey, were presumably left undivided.

Like all Norman "donjons," the White Tower, though uncomfortable, was immensely strong. No attacker could hope to scale the ninety-foot walls, or to pierce through them without spending a great deal of time and effort. The store-rooms in the basement (where there was also a cell in the south-west corner) could hold provisions against a long siege, and a few men could hold a small doorway, raised fifteen feet above the ground and approached by a wooden stair, against an army. On the other hand, the very thickness of the walls and the inaccessibility of the door made it impossible for the defenders to sally out and attack the enemies. From the battlements round the roof they could fire missiles, or drop stones and boiling oil when the enemy came close under the walls, and they could also shoot from the loopholes (which were later enlarged to make windows). Apart from this, "their strength was to sit still," until their friends came to their relief or the besiegers gave up.

Besides its state apartments, living quarters and store-rooms, the White Tower contains, at the south-east corner of the third floor, St. John's Chapel, plain but beautiful in the Norman style, with short, solid columns carrying thirteen round arches and separating the central nave from the aisles. The nave is roofed by a plain barrel vault thirty-two feet above its floor, at the height of the ceiling of the fourth storey. But the vaults of the side aisles are no higher than the ceilings of the other rooms of the third storey, and above them a sort of gallery, called a triforium, runs round the north, east and south of the chapel, with arched openings looking down into the nave.

The chapel is reached by a small door on its north side, and also by a passage in the thickness of the south wall, which leads to the great chamber on the west side of the Tower, and to the head of a corkscrew stair, going down to the floor below   where the original door to the tower was probably situated. It was at the foot of this stair that in 1674 were found the bones of two children, supposed to be the "Princes in the Tower," the child-king Edward V and his brother, murdered by their uncle and "Protector" Richard Duke of Gloucester in 1483.

On the top floor of the Tower is the great council chamber to which the young King's supporter Lord Hastings, secure, as he thought, in Richard's favour, went in spite of all unlucky signs and the advice of his friends —

> Stanley did dream the boar did raze his helm;
> And I did scorn it, and disdain'd to fly.
> Three times today my foot-cloth horse did stumble,
> And started when he looked upon the Tower,
> As loath to bear me to the slaughter-house.

In the morning he had been rejoicing over the deaths of his enemies; by dinner time he was dead himself by Richard's orders —

> Off with his head! Now, by Saint Paul I swear,
> I will not dine until I see the same.

After the death of Hastings the tragedy of the Princes followed swiftly—

> The mose arch deed of piteous massacre
> That ever yet this land was guilty of.

Down to our own time the history of the Tower of London is largely a list of state prisoners and executions. (As recently as the Second World War, Rudolph Hess, Hitler's Deputy, was imprisoned in the Tower, and at least one German spy was shot there.) However, many of these sad stories are not concerned specially with the White Tower, but with the lesser towers in the two concentric lines of defence that have been added to the fortress from the beginning of the thirteenth century on.

The
White
Tower

Southwest Tower

Roof platform fits here

Paste West Wall along here

Roof Platform fits here

Paste South Wall along here

Southwest   Tower

3. Southwest Tower (Square)

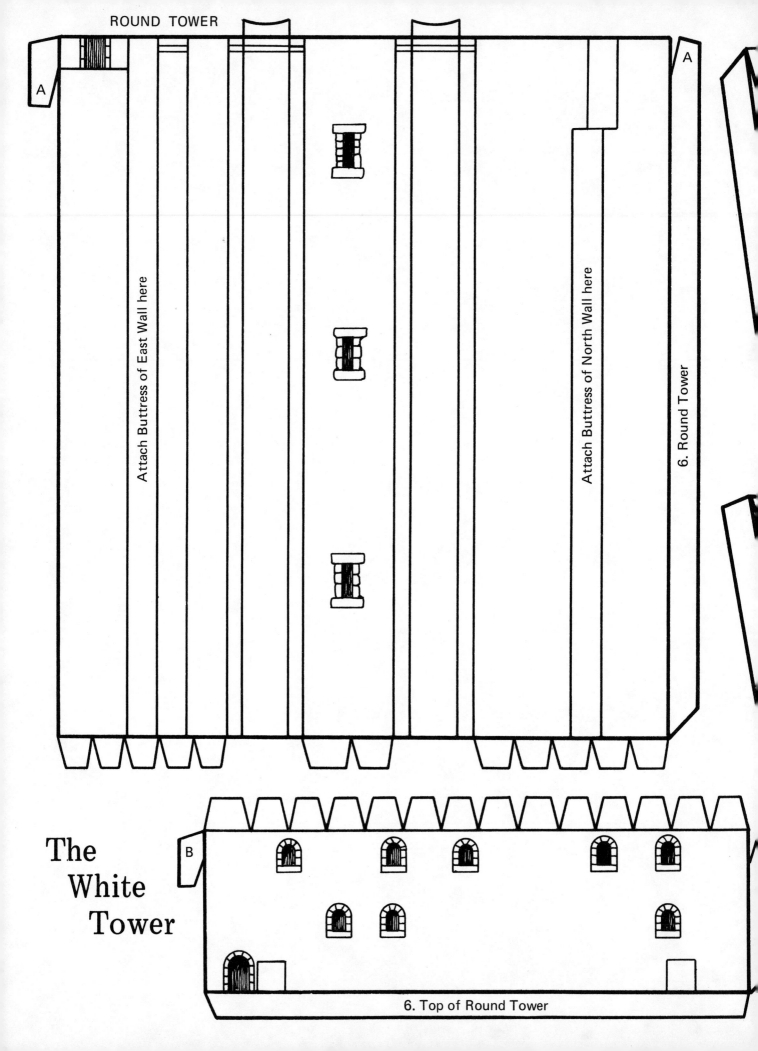

ROUND TOWER

A

A

Attach Buttress of East Wall here

Attach Buttress of North Wall here

6. Round Tower

The
White
Tower

B

6. Top of Round Tower

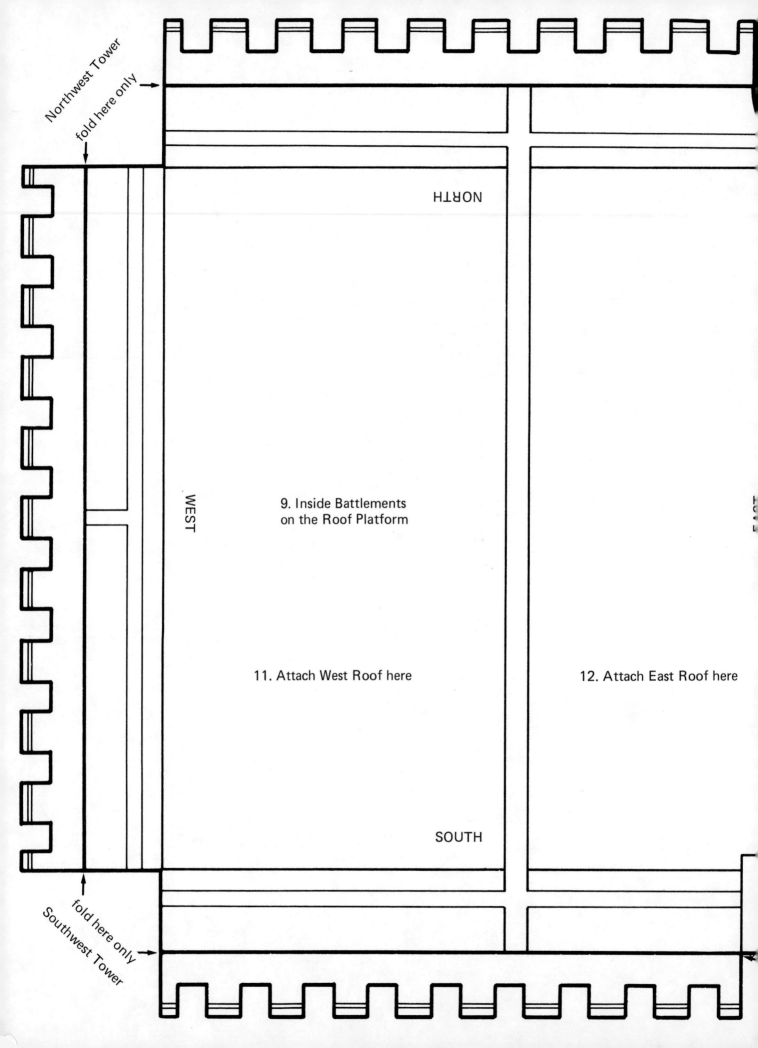

fold here only

NORTH

WEST

9. Inside Battlements
on the Roof Platform

11. Attach West Roof here

12. Attach East Roof here

SOUTH

fold here only

Southwest Tower

The White Tower

WEST WALL

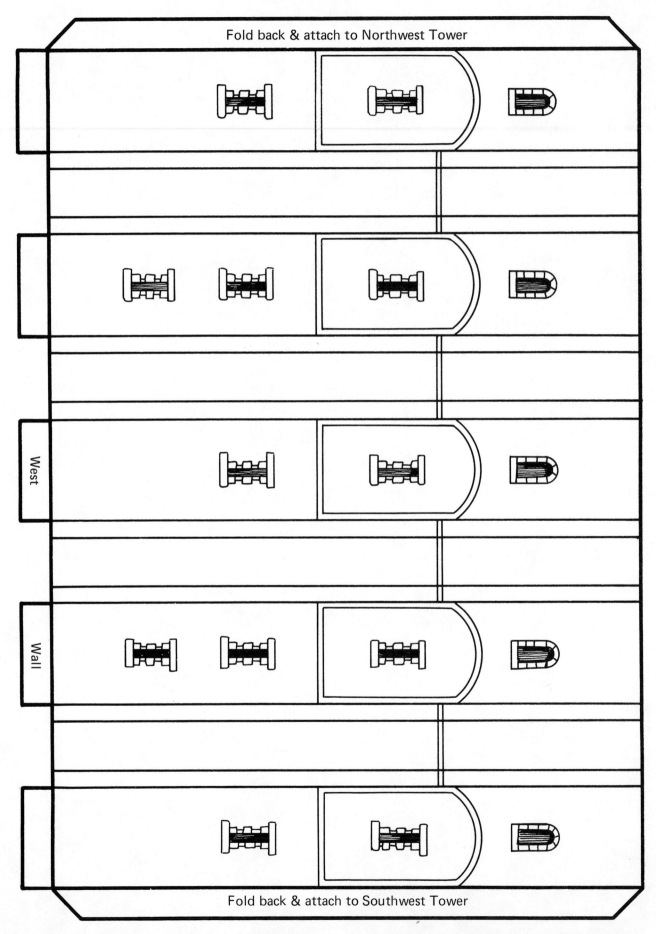

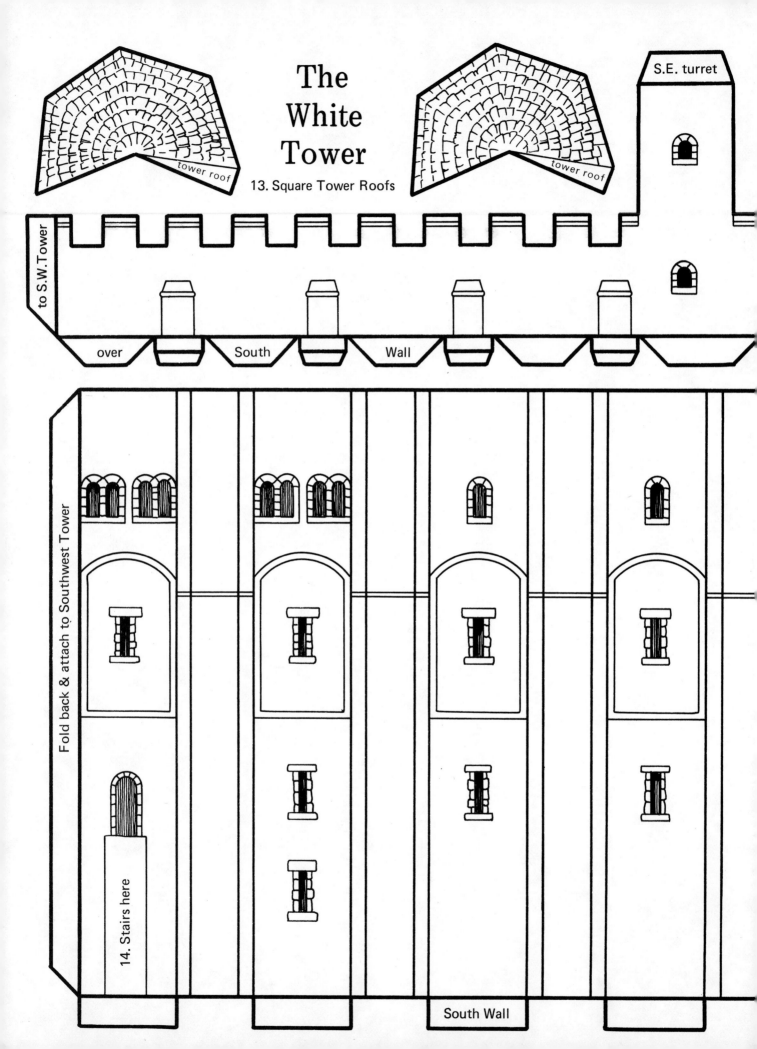

The White Tower

13. Square Tower Roofs

tower roof

tower roof

S.E. turret

to S.W. Tower

over   South   Wall

Fold back & attach to Southwest Tower

14. Stairs here

South Wall

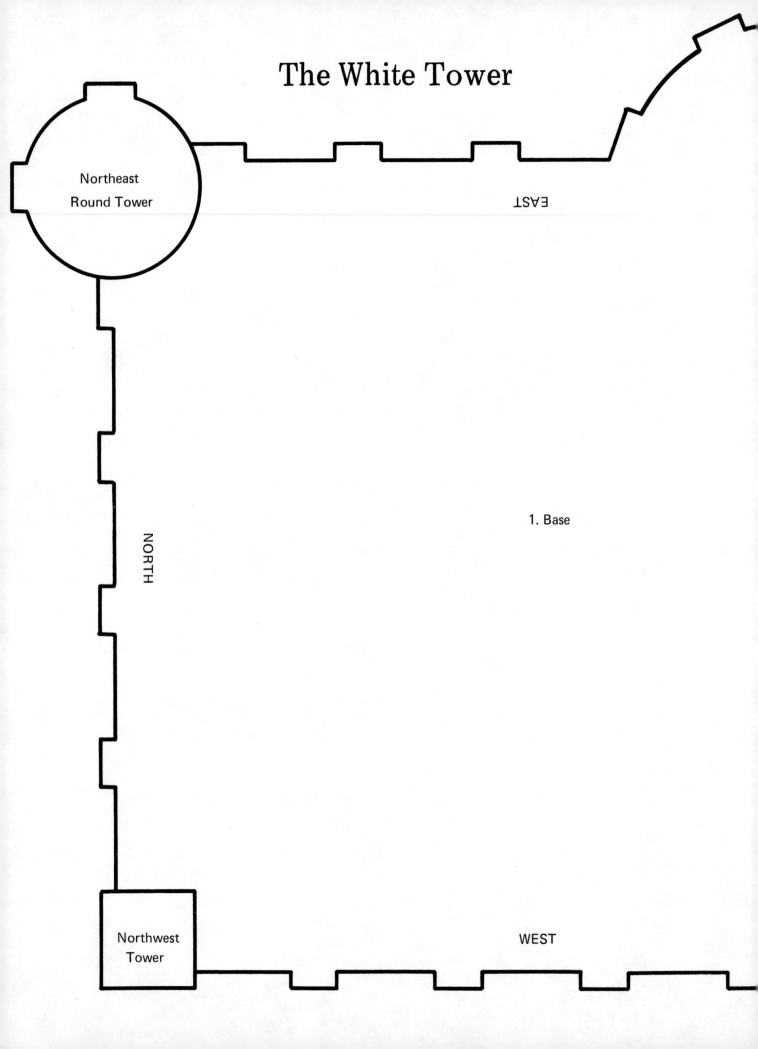

The White Tower

Northeast
Round Tower

EAST

NORTH

1. Base

Northwest
Tower

WEST

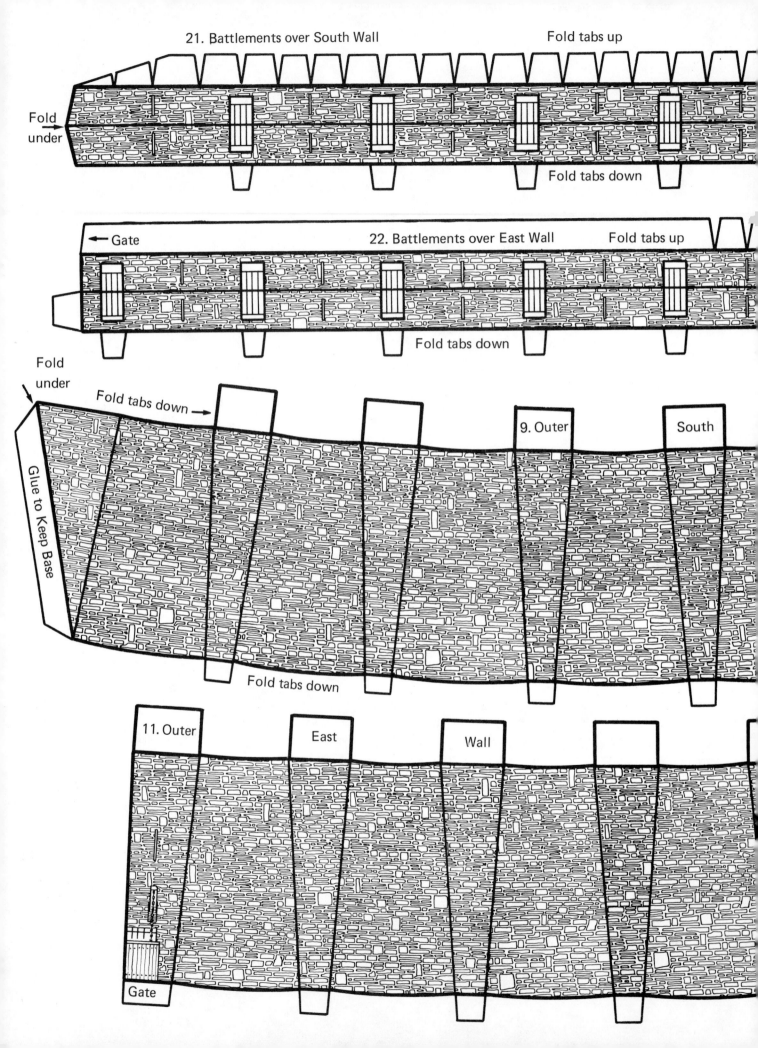

21. Battlements over South Wall

Fold tabs up

Fold under

Fold tabs down

← Gate

22. Battlements over East Wall

Fold tabs up

Fold tabs down

Fold under

Fold tabs down →

Glue to Keep Base

9. Outer

South

Fold tabs down

11. Outer

East

Wall

Gate

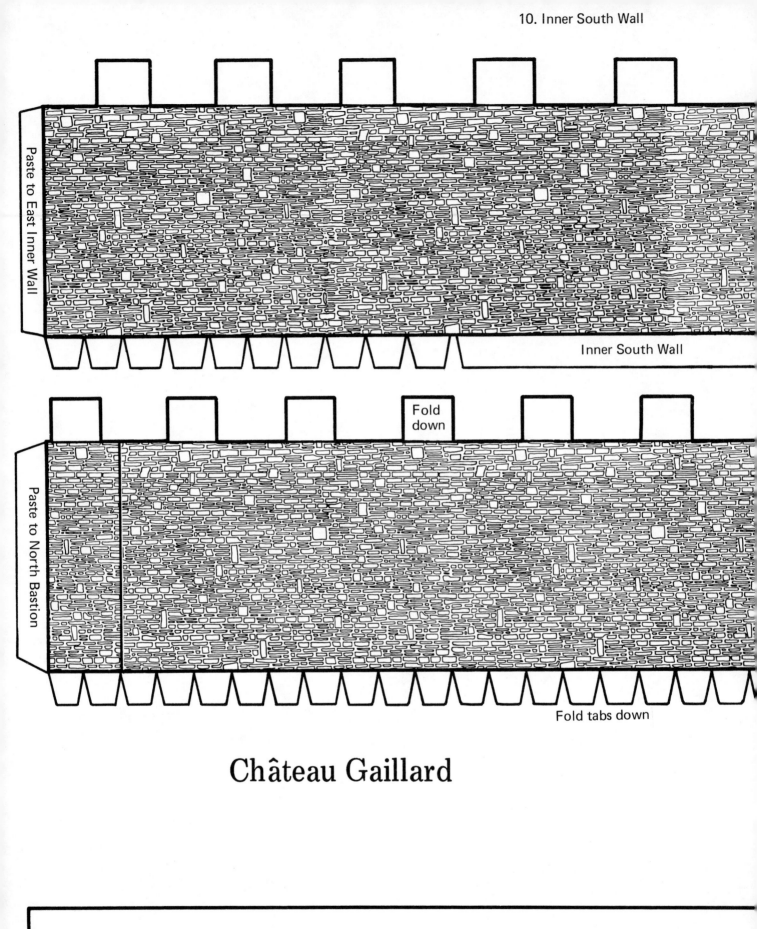

Paste to East Inner Wall

Inner South Wall

Fold down

Paste to North Bastion

Fold tabs down

Château Gaillard

20. Floor over East Wall

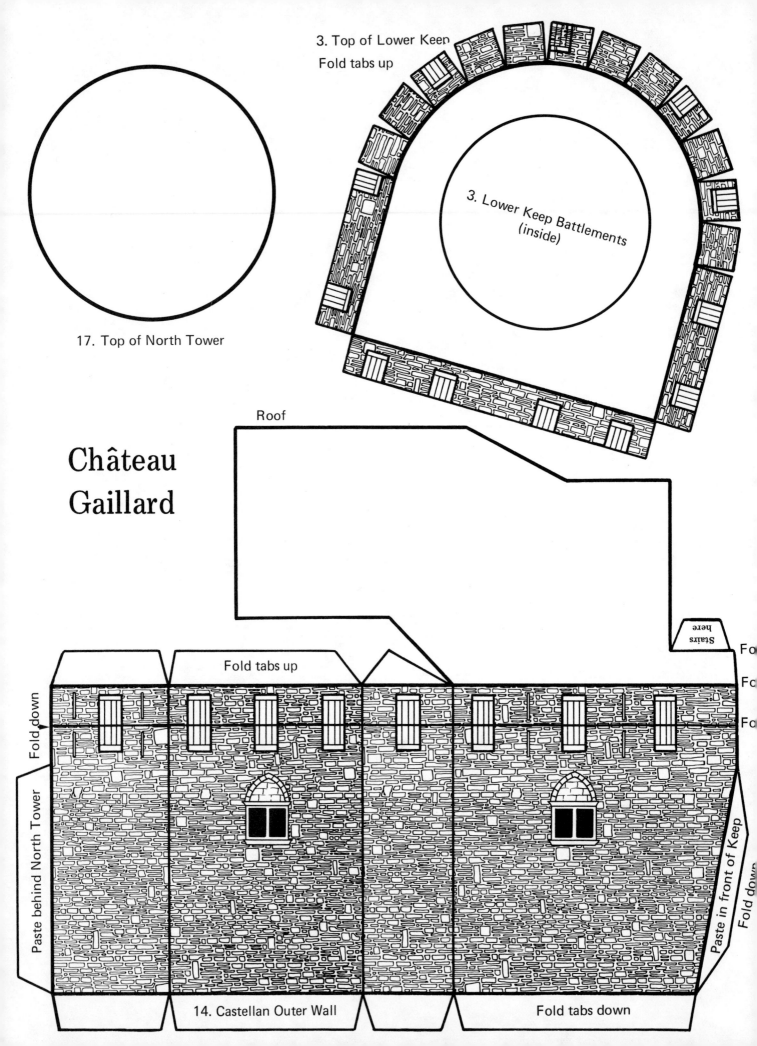

3. Top of Lower Keep

Fold tabs up

3. Lower Keep Battlements (inside)

17. Top of North Tower

Roof

Château Gaillard

Stairs here

Fold tabs up

Fold down

Paste behind North Tower

Paste in front of Keep

Fold down

14. Castellan Outer Wall

Fold tabs down

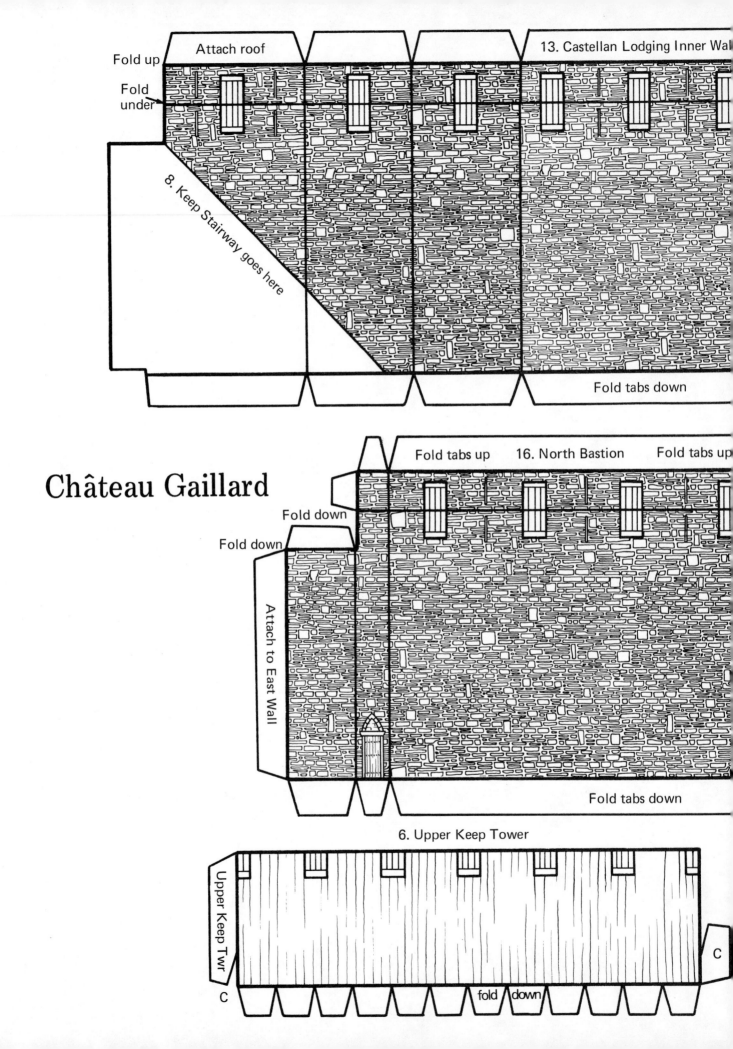

Château Gaillard

Château Gaillard

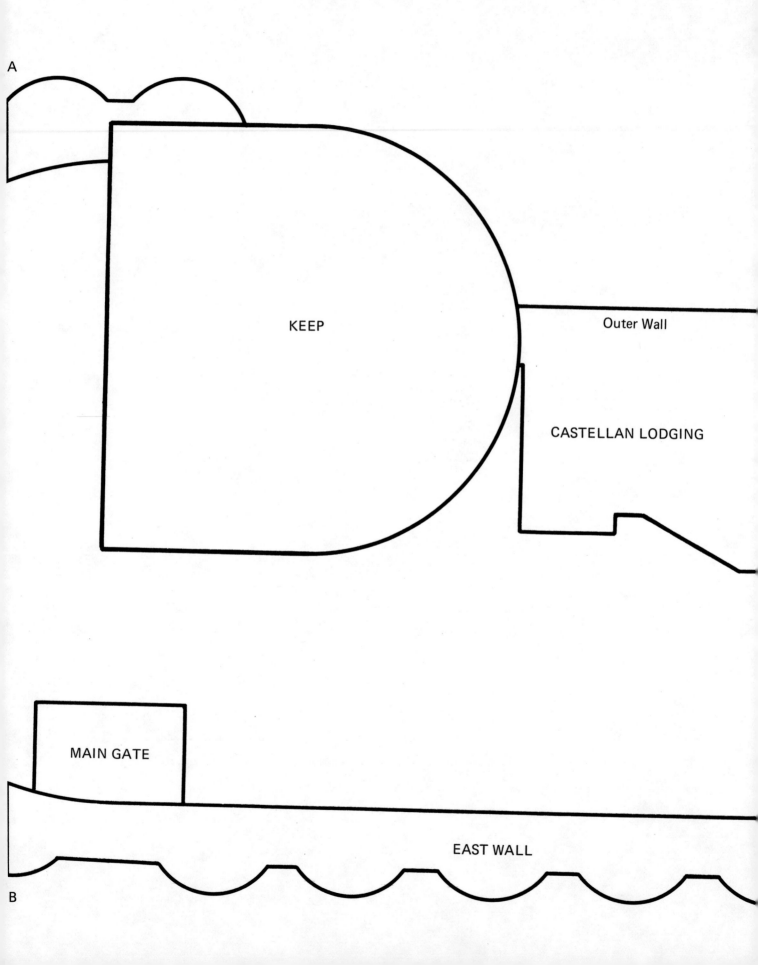

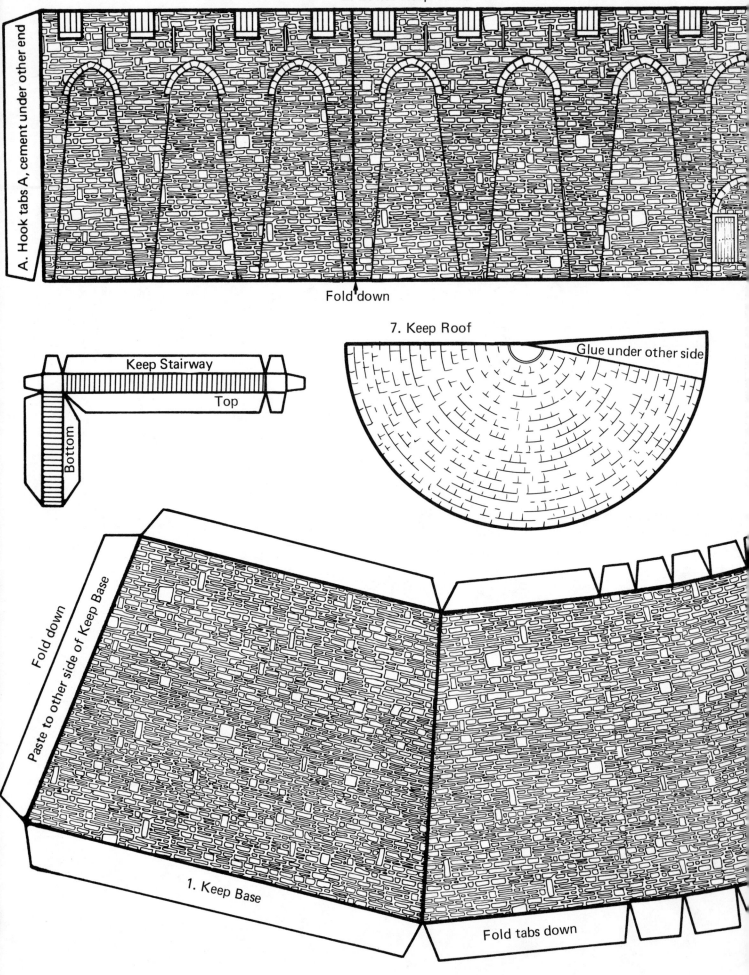

2. Lower Keep Tower

A. Hook tabs A, cement under other end

Fold down

7. Keep Roof

Glue under other side

Keep Stairway

Top

Bottom

Fold down

Paste to other side of Keep Base

1. Keep Base

Fold tabs down

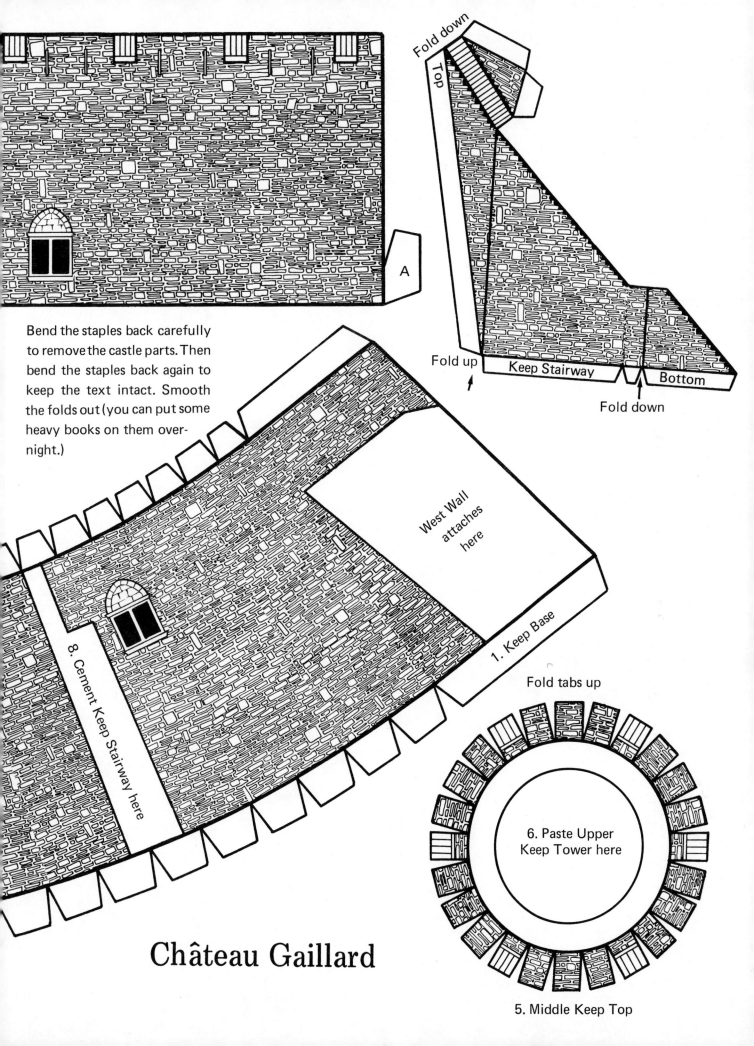

Bend the staples back carefully to remove the castle parts. Then bend the staples back again to keep the text intact. Smooth the folds out (you can put some heavy books on them overnight.)

A

Fold down

Top

Fold up

Keep Stairway

Bottom

Fold down

West Wall attaches here

1. Keep Base

Fold tabs up

8. Cement Keep Stairway here

6. Paste Upper Keep Tower here

5. Middle Keep Top

Château Gaillard

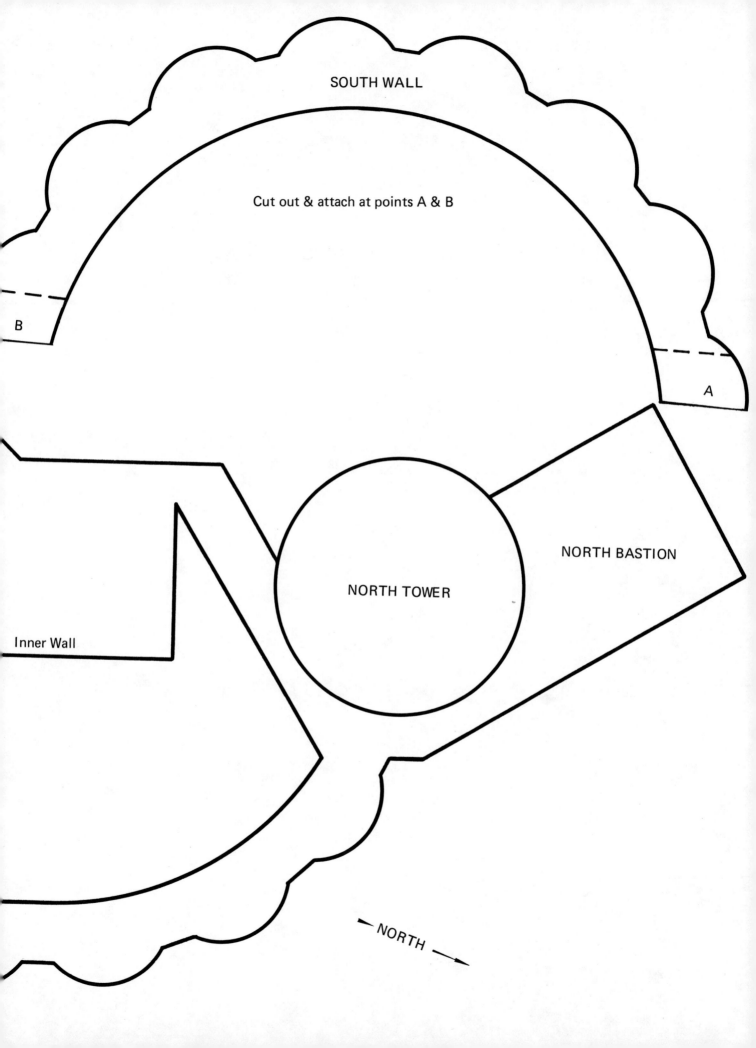

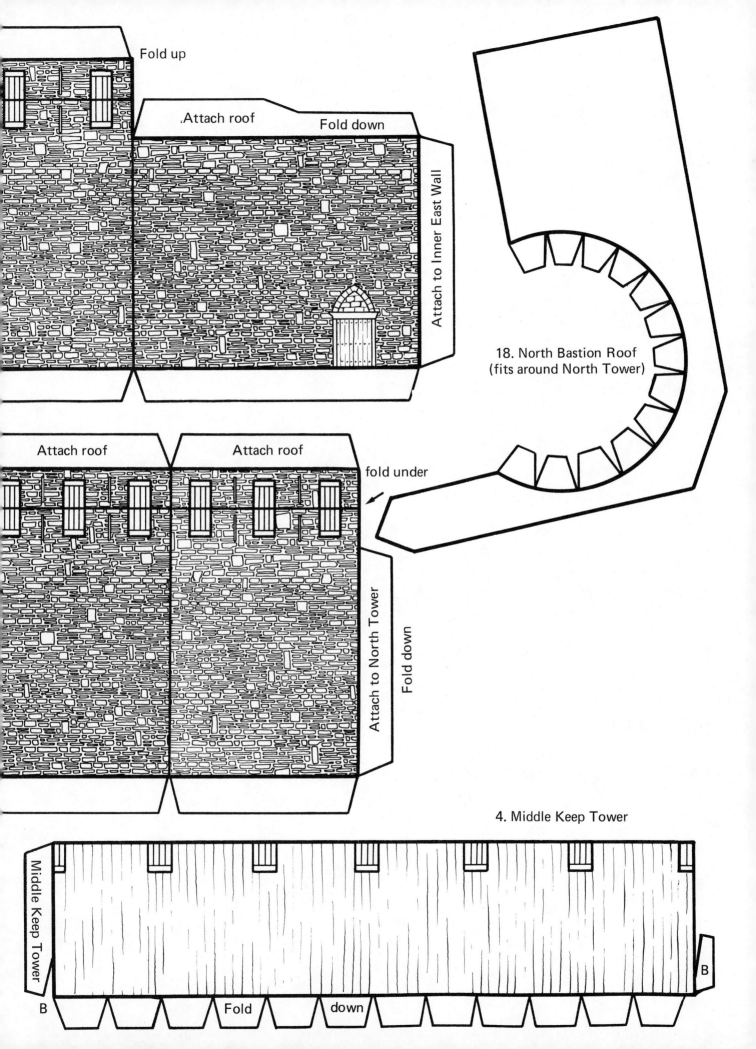

Fold up

.Attach roof   Fold down

Attach to Inner East Wall

18. North Bastion Roof
(fits around North Tower)

Attach roof   Attach roof

fold under

Attach to North Tower

Fold down

4. Middle Keep Tower

Middle Keep Tower

B

Fold   down

B

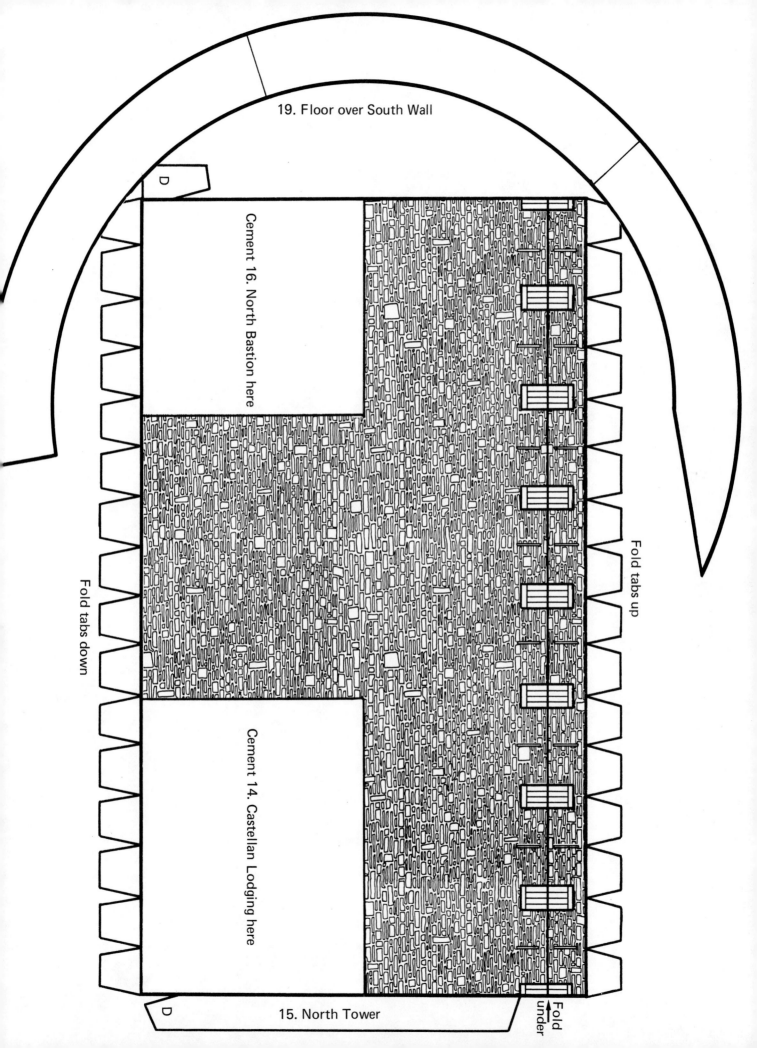

19. Floor over South Wall

D

Cement 16. North Bastion here

Fold tabs up

Fold tabs down

Cement 14. Castellan Lodging here

D

15. North Tower

Fold under

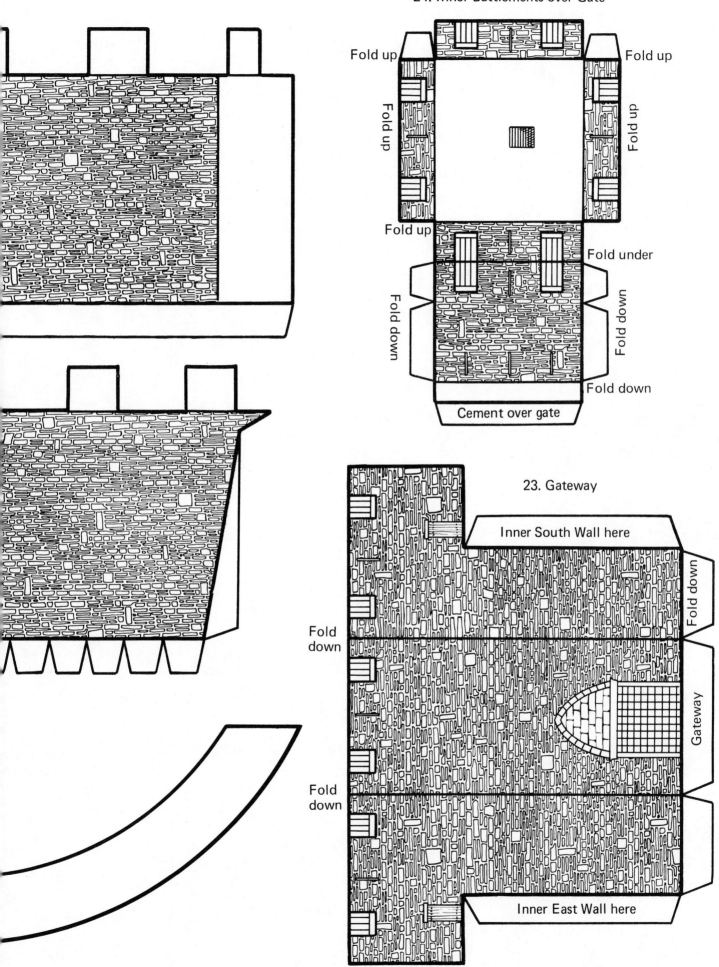

24. Inner Battlements over Gate

Fold up

Fold up

Fold up

Fold up

Fold up

Fold under

Fold down

Fold down

Fold down

Fold down

Cement over gate

23. Gateway

Inner South Wall here

Fold down

Fold down

Fold down

Gateway

Inner East Wall here

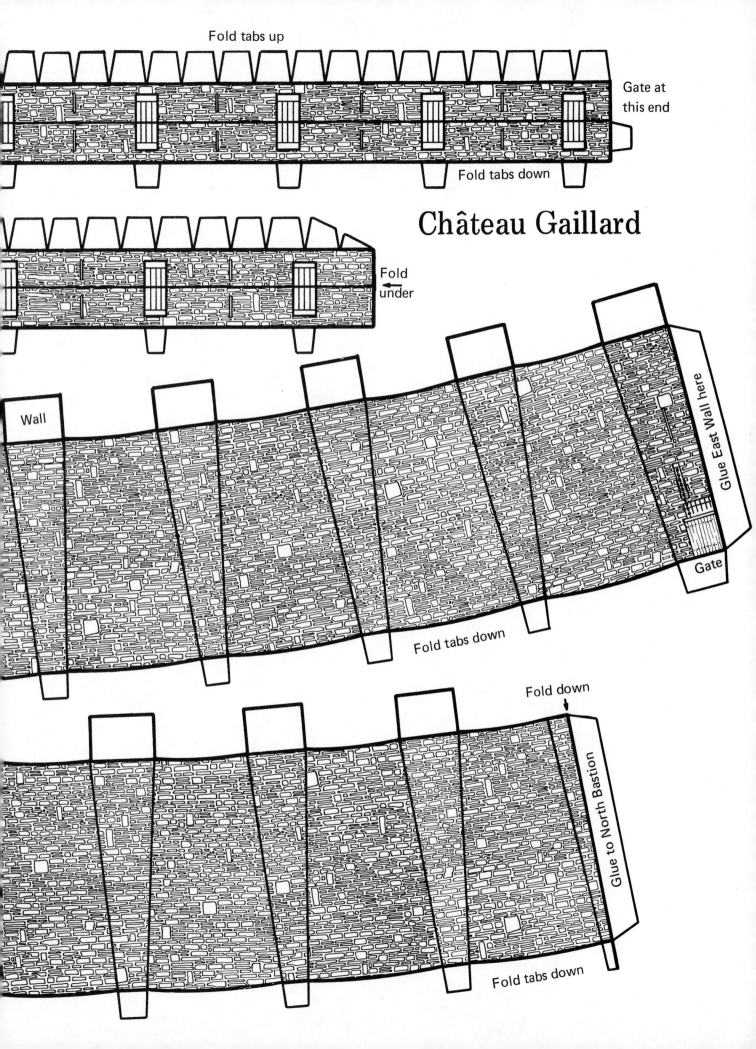

Fold tabs up

Gate at this end

Fold tabs down

Fold under

Château Gaillard

Wall

Glue East Wall here

Fold tabs down

Gate

Fold down

Glue to North Bastion

Fold tabs down

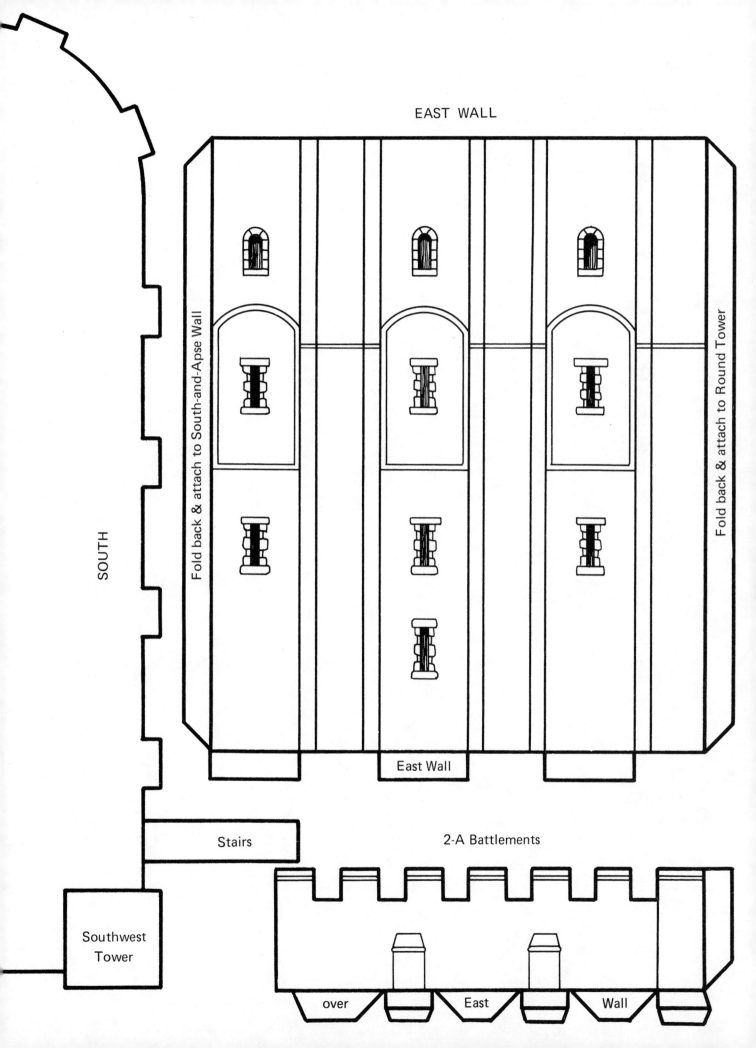

EAST WALL

SOUTH

Fold back & attach to South-and-Apse Wall

Fold back & attach to Round Tower

East Wall

Stairs

2-A Battlements

Southwest Tower

over   East   Wall

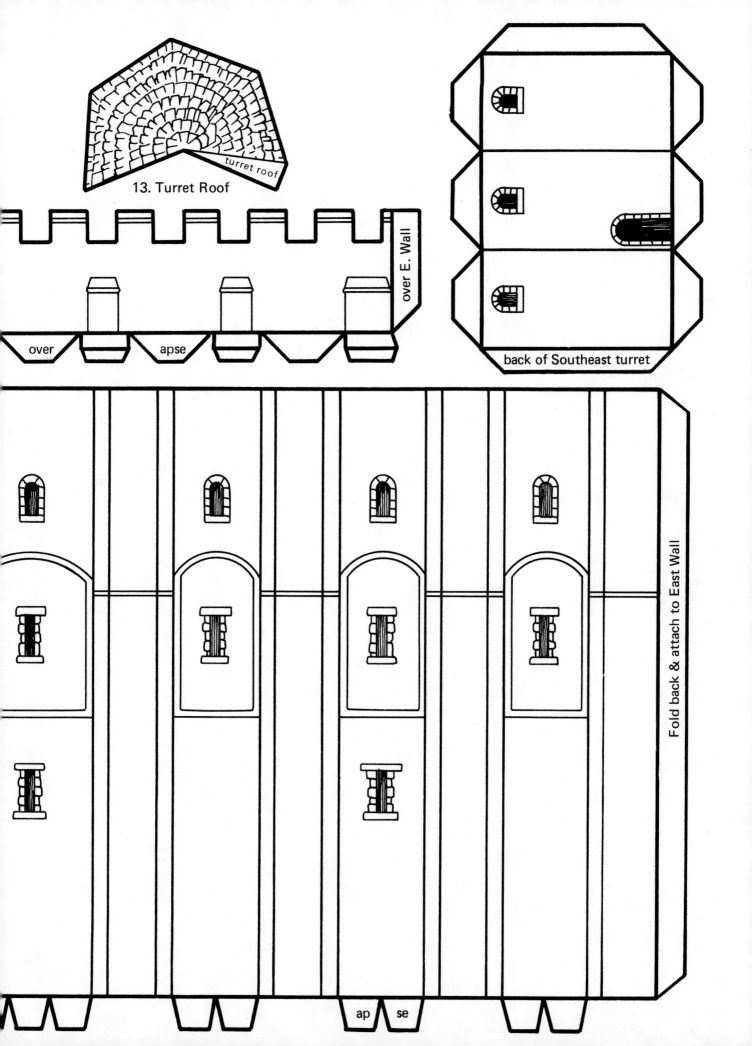

13. Turret Roof

turret roof

over E. Wall

over   apse

back of Southeast turret

Fold back & attach to East Wall

ap se

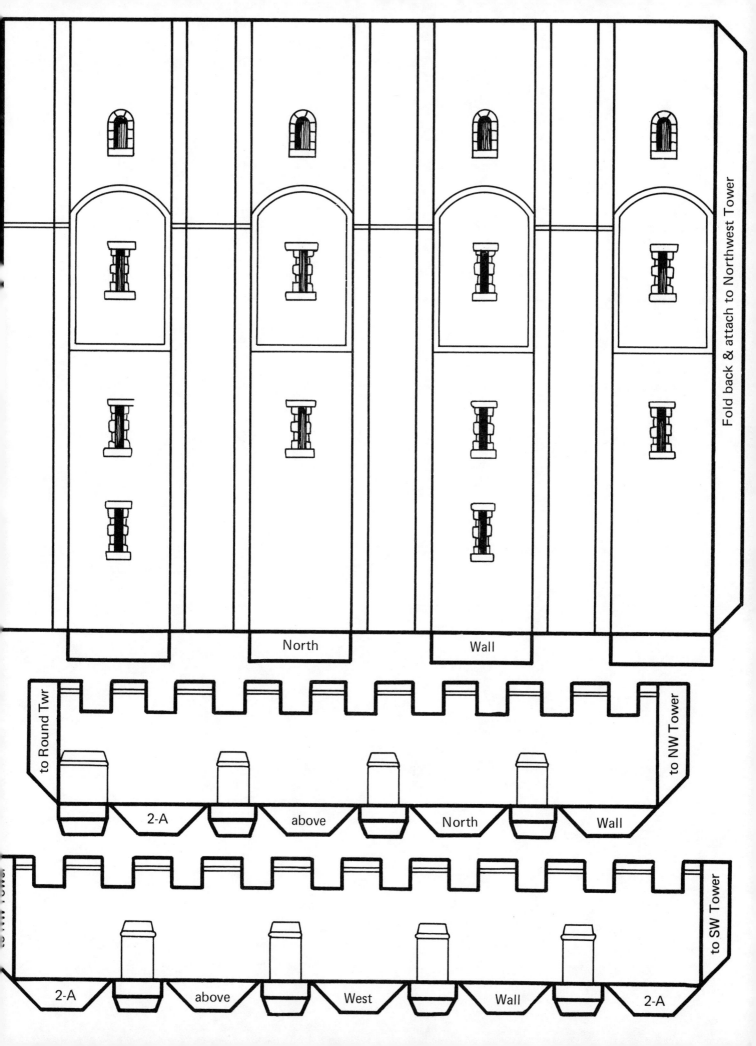

Fold back & attach to Northwest Tower

North   Wall

to Round Twr

to NW Tower

2-A   above   North   Wall

to SW Tower

2-A   above   West   Wall   2-A

The White Tower

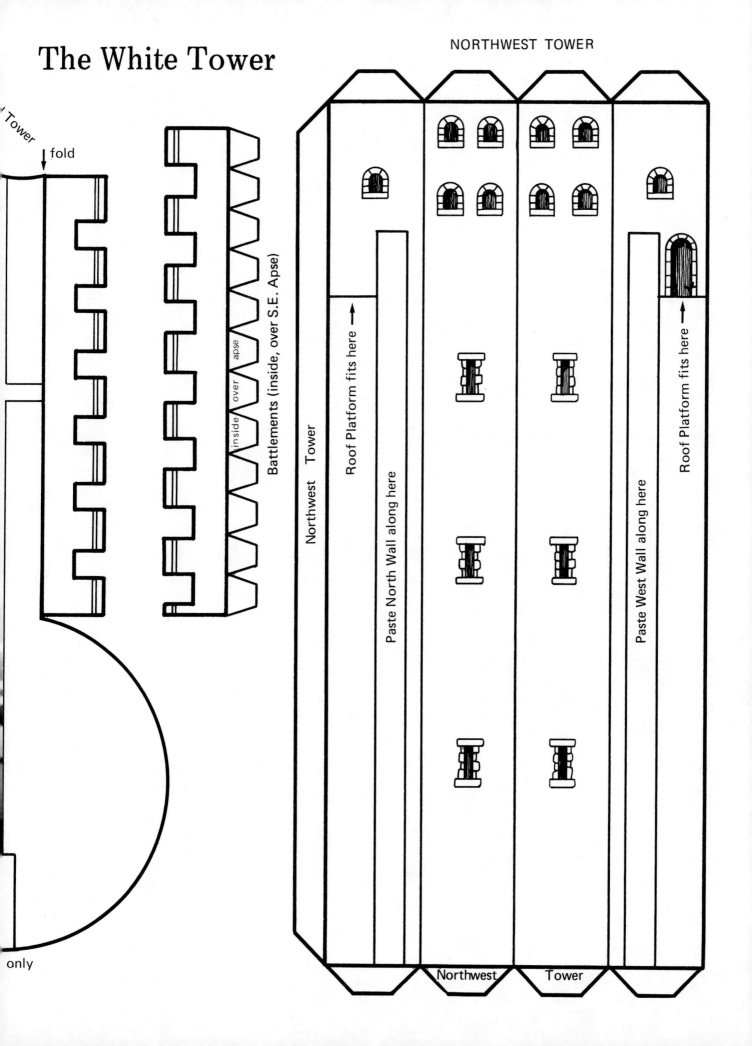

fold

Tower

only

Battlements (inside, over S.E. Apse)

inside over apse

Northwest Tower

Roof Platform fits here →

Paste North Wall along here

Paste West Wall along here

Roof Platform fits here →

Northwest   Tower

11. West Roof

12. East Roof

6. Round Tower Roof

Round Tower Roof

To South Wall

14. Stairs

The old song says that Ann Boleyn "walks the Bloody Tower," but I can find no convincing report of her being seen

With her head tucked underneath her arm
At the midnight hour.

Besides, even as a prisoner she was given the same comfortable quarters in the Lieutenant's Lodging that she had had when she came in state to the Tower just before her coronation. But the Bloody Tower, at the entrance to the Inner Ward, did hold many distinguished prisoners—the Protestant martyrs Latimer, Cranmer and Ridley in Bloody Mary's time; under James I, Sir Walter Raleigh. "Nobody but my father would keep such an eagle in such a cage," said Prince Henry, who might have saved Raleigh if he had not died young.

In the Beauchamp Tower—named for the Earl of Warwick imprisoned by Richard II—are hundreds of inscriptions cut on the walls by later prisoners. When Queen Elizabeth I finally lost patience with her conceited and headstrong favourite "Robin"—Robert Devereux, Earl of Essex—she put him in "Robin the Devil's Tower," which has been the Devereux Tower ever since. In the basement of the Bell Tower is the cell where Sir Thomas More was confined. Saint Thomas's Tower contains the famous "Traitor's Gate"—the water-gate through which passed prisoners arrested at Westminster and brought by boat down the Thames to avoid the City of London, whose citizens were often unfriendly to the royal authority.

Besides human prisoners, the Tower contained the royal menagerie, which for hundreds of years was shown to visitors on payment of a small fee. Lions—suggesting the "lions in the Capitol" of Shakespeare's Julius Caesar—were always there, until the opening of the Zoo in Regent's Park in 1835 provided them with better quarters. Sometimes there were greater rarities. Matthew Paris, the historian of Henry III's reign, records an elephant, a present from the King of France (unfortunately it died in 1258, only a few years after its arrival). A little earlier, Henry had had a Polar bear, for whose keep the sheriffs of London were required to pay fourpence (silver pennies!) a day, and provide a long chain so that it could go fishing off Tower Wharf. (In those days the salmon still ran up

"The silver Thames between his gardens green.")

Of all these animals, only the Tower Ravens are left, with an official allowance for their keep, in the care of one of the Yeomen of the Guard, who is named the Raven Master.

Château Gaillard

Château Gaillard, the "Saucy Castle," built in 1196 by Richard the Lion Heart to guard Rouen, the capital of Normandy, from attacks down the River Seine, shows how the art of fortification in western Europe was changed by what the Crusaders had seen in the Holy Land.

The castle stands three hundred feet above the river, on a precipitous mass of rock, at whose feet lie the twin towns of Les Andelys, which Richard also fortified. The land belonged to the Archbishop of Rouen, who hurried to Rome to complain when the King seized it. Heaven seemed to back the Archbishop's protest when a rain of blood fell on Richard and his workmen. But, says an old chronicler, if an angel had come down to stay the King's hand he would have met with no answer but a curse. So quickly was the work pushed on that within a twelvemonth Richard called his barons together to admire the beauty of his "year-old daughter."

Philip Augustus, King of France and overlord of the Duchy of Normandy, Richard's former fellow-crusader and bitter enemy, saw the castle when the kings met for a conference on an island in the Seine. He swore to conquer it even if its walls had been built of iron, and Richard replied that even if they had been built of butter he could hold the castle against Philip and all his army.

The great donjon tower, or keep, is still the heart of the castle. But the defenders were no longer meant to shelter within it and trust to the strength of its walls. Three lines of fortification had to be overcome one after the other before the attackers could reach the keep, and each line was planned for an active defence supported by flanking fire from crossbows and stone-throwing catapults. First, on the narrow neck that joined the castle rock to the hills above the Seine, was built a great round tower, from either side of which a curtain wall runs back obliquely. Each curtain ends in another great tower, and has a smaller tower half way along it, and a third wall completes the enclosure, so that the whole work is in the form of a triangle pointing towards the direction from which attack must come. Outside it was dug a ditch forty feet deep, with sheer sides.

Behind the base of the triangle a second ditch guards a rampart eight feet thick, with more round towers at its corners. Then comes a third ditch, guarding the inmost ward, which, though the smallest of the three, is still over sixty yards long and thirty wide. On the south-west this is protected by the cliffs falling to the river, down which ran stairways connecting outworks, and about its other sides curls a massive wall, over five hundred feet long. From its face project seventeen great rounded buttresses, each almost touching its neighbour, so that almost all the ground at the foot of the wall could be covered by cross-fire from the top of these projections.

Behind the wall stands the great keep—a round tower, forty-eight feet in diameter, but appearing to be square on the side facing the inner ward, which is shielded by a great triangular spur of solid masonry. The walls are eleven feet thick, of small stones and flints set in concrete, but faced with squared blocks. They are "battered"—that is, their outer face is not perpendicular, but sloped steeply for two thirds of its height. This makes the base thicker. Above the batter rise massive stone buttresses which probably carried an overhanging gallery of stone or wood, whose floor would have been pierced to allow the defenders to drop missiles without exposing themselves. These missiles would have been deflected outwards by the batter, and it would have been hard for attackers to shelter directly under the wall.

Floors and stairs within the tower have vanished. They must have been made of wood. There are no rooms set within the thickness of the wall; no fireplaces: and no "garderobes" or lavatories. So the tower clearly did not serve as living quarters in peacetime. The governor of the castle probably lived in a rectangular building whose ruins lie next to the keep. Other residential buildings, including, as we shall see, a chapel built by Richard's successor John, stood in the other wards.

Richard died in 1199. In August 1203 Philip attacked Château Gaillard. The defence had been entrusted by John, whose Norman barons were turning against him, to a veteran soldier brought from England, Roger de Lacy, Constable of Chester. The French forced their way across the Seine, beat back an attempt to relieve the fortress, and stormed the island tower and the two towns of Les Andelys. But the "Saucy Castle" on its cliffs still defied Philip. All winter long his army blockaded it from their entrenchments, while the refugees from Les Andelys, whom de Lacy had turned out of the castle and the French would not allow to pass, starved miserably between the lines. Finally the assault began. Philip's engineers brought up a high wooden tower and mobile shelters to cover the filling of the ditch. "But the besieged too defended themselves no less stoutly," says William the Breton, the French chronicler, "using stone-throwing catapults and mangonels, with which they hindered and caused loss to our men, and killed many of our people

Château Gaillard

Château Gaillard

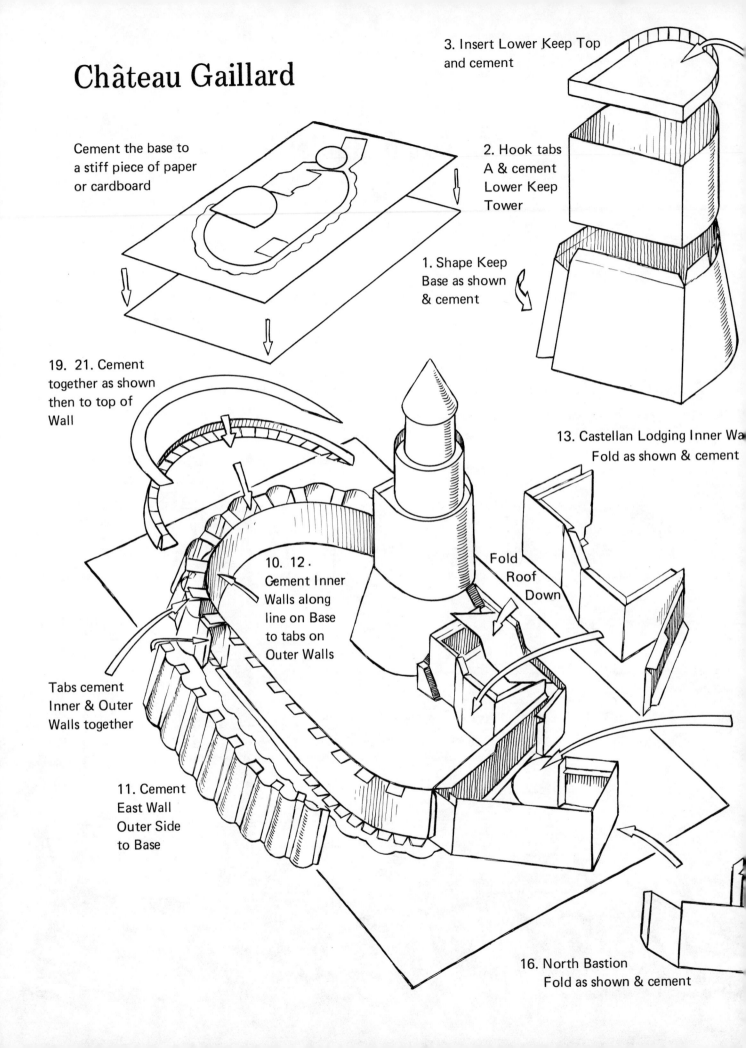

Cement the base to a stiff piece of paper or cardboard

3. Insert Lower Keep Top and cement

2. Hook tabs A & cement Lower Keep Tower

1. Shape Keep Base as shown & cement

19. 21. Cement together as shown then to top of Wall

13. Castellan Lodging Inner Wa Fold as shown & cement

Fold Roof Down

10. 12. Cement Inner Walls along line on Base to tabs on Outer Walls

Tabs cement Inner & Outer Walls together

11. Cement East Wall Outer Side to Base

16. North Bastion Fold as shown & cement

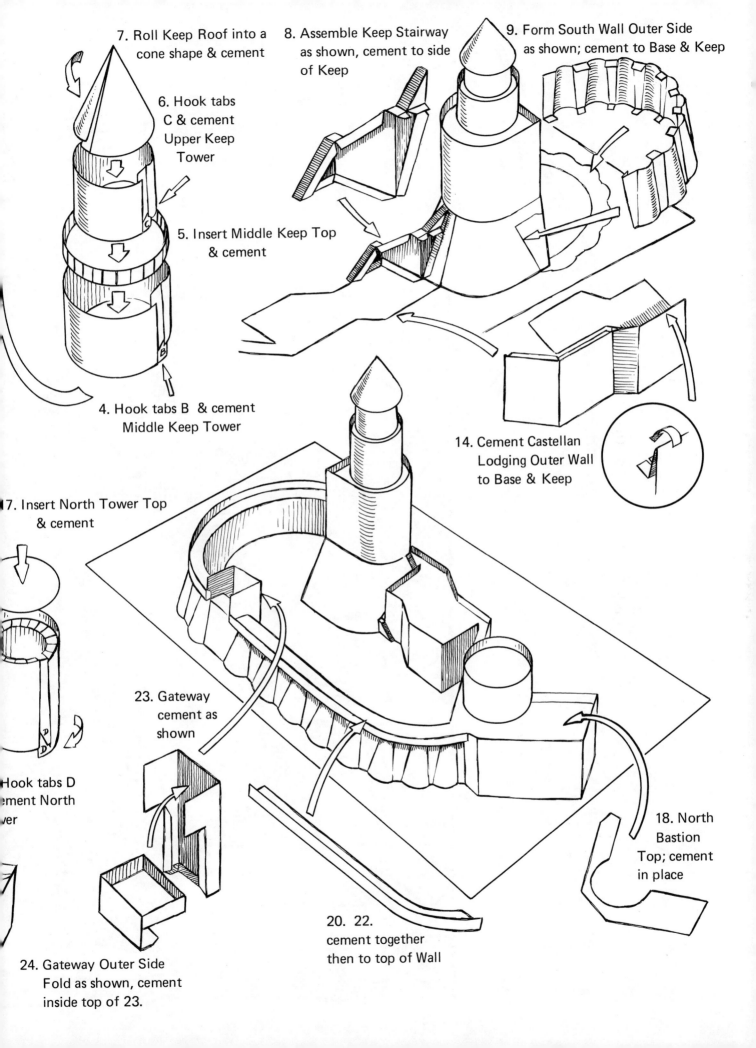

7. Roll Keep Roof into a cone shape & cement

6. Hook tabs C & cement Upper Keep Tower

8. Assemble Keep Stairway as shown, cement to side of Keep

9. Form South Wall Outer Side as shown; cement to Base & Keep

5. Insert Middle Keep Top & cement

4. Hook tabs B & cement Middle Keep Tower

14. Cement Castellan Lodging Outer Wall to Base & Keep

17. Insert North Tower Top & cement

Hook tabs D cement North Tower

23. Gateway cement as shown

18. North Bastion Top; cement in place

24. Gateway Outer Side Fold as shown, cement inside top of 23.

20. 22. cement together then to top of Wall

An assault from about the time
of the building of Château Gaillard

From a mid-13th century manuscript in the Pierpont Morgan Library

with cross-bow bolts, and with stones hurled from their mangonels."

At last, when the ditch was half-filled, the French scrambled down into it by scaling ladders, covering themselves with their shields, then placed the same ladders against the inner edge of the ditch and gained a position from which they could undermine the base of the great advanced tower. They propped it on wooden supports until their work was done. Then they fired the wood and made their way back by the way they had come. The tower collapsed: its ruins filled the ditch, and the defenders retreated, burning the buildings in the outer enclosure behind them. "When the fire died down we won the first line, but the second presented great difficulties. However, King John had erected a lofty chapel, rising above the walls, adjoining the walls themselves, next to the latrines, thereby committing, as it seemed, an offense against religion. A window appeared above the wall on the east side, and Peter Snub (as we used to nickname him from the shortness of his nose), a young man of the highest character and approved valor, after making a reconnaissance with a few companions, found that the ditch was shallower on the side nearest the river. He crossed and made his way to the window, but could not reach it without a scaling-ladder. So he climbed up on the bent back of one of his friends and jumped for it; reached the window with his hand; and, after hanging for a long time, made his entrance with wonderful agility. Then, letting down a rope, he drew his friends up to him. When the besieged saw what had happened, they fired the chapel and all the buildings, and retreated within the third line, in which was the keep, leaving the second abandoned to us. We thought that Peter and his companions had perished in the flames, but they hid in the crypt until the fire died down."

Across the third ditch Richard had left a causeway of rock, and so the French were able to bring up shelters for their sappers, covered by the fire of a great stone-throwing catapult. "And a breach was opened, through which our knights and men-at-arms entered, and they captured all whom they found within, forty knights and a hundred and twenty men-at-arms, and many others." (Not one of the defenders, we are told elsewhere, would surrender, but every one had to be overcome and disarmed by main force. It is interesting that there was no last stand in the keep, after the wall in front of it was breached.)

"Thus within three weeks King Philip won all Château Gaillard, and he re-fortified it wonderfully, and kept it for himself, placing in it a garrison and abundant provisions."